How to Analyze People

Understanding the Human Psychology,Human Behavior,Reading People, and Their Body Language

Lawrence Franz

Table of Contents

Introduction

Have you ever walked away from a conversation with the feeling that the person to whom you were speaking was not being entirely open and honest with you—or that there was a general disconnect between the words spoken and the impression that they left you with? Do you wish that you could pinpoint exactly why?

In the workplace, have you ever struggled with asserting authority over your employees? Or have you wondered how to figure out and approach your aloof boss so that you can present an important idea to them, with the hope of professional advancement? Do you wish that you had better skills in understanding and communicating with colleagues?

At home, with family or friends, do you sometimes feel that you are just not on the same page with someone you care about, that you can never seem to say the right thing at the right time to avoid conflict and confrontation? Do you wish that you could see into people, with a sort of X-Ray vision to understand their wants and expectations?

If you have ever wished any of those things, you can benefit from learning to read people to determine their personality types and the meanings behind their nonverbal expressions in communication. This book can help you do precisely that.

The modern world is complex, complicated, and fraught with the near-constant potential and risk of miscommunication and conflict. All but the most isolated individuals have daily interactions with a diverse range of people possessing different backgrounds, perspectives, ways of thinking, and ways of verbally expressing themselves. Even when people share the same language, not everyone shares (or uses) the same vocabulary in the same way, due to cultural differences, personal experiences, and individual agendas.

Effective and productive communication is critical in all areas of life—personal and professional, private and public—not only for preventing conflict and maintaining harmonious relationships but also for achieving success, attaining goals, and what we think of as "getting ahead." In some cases, good communication skills assist in, or are even necessary for, protecting yourself and your interests from exploitation and harm.

Given the highly important role of interpersonal communication, understanding, and learning to read how people reveal their personalities and nonverbal expressions of meaning can be beneficial to all areas of life.

Communicating with others is some kind of a journey—an interactive path through a landscape of meanings, messages, and negotiations, with the (hopefully!) eventual destination point of mutual understanding and agreement or, at the very least, amicable and constructive disagreement.

With the idea of conversational exchange being a journey, this book will offer a roadmap and navigational tool for identifying and interpreting the signs and signals of nonverbal expressions in others, as well as in yourself. It will also serve as something of a "travel guide" through the different interpersonal territories of gender, the professional arena and workplace, and the greater world at large—assisting you in comprehending the effect of context in communication so that you may utilize your skill in reading body language in the best and most appropriate manner.

There are many books and resources available on this subject on the market—thank you again for selecting this one! Every effort was put forth to ensure that all of the information within it is as accurate, relevant, and as useful as possible. Please enjoy!

Chapter 1 – The Psychology of Communication Behaviors

People Need People

Human beings are social creatures. While some individuals are inclined towards introversion and prefer to limit interactions with others whenever possible, the general thrust of humanity leans towards sociability and connecting with each other in a common, shared space of mutual activity and existence.

Even in the earliest days after the emergence of *homo sapiens* as a distinct and unique species, mankind has consistently displayed a preference, even a need, for gathering together into groups. The foundation and the core of all forms of human social groups is communication. In any type of human collective, be it a family or a civilization, living with and among other people requires a constant exchange of information, a persistent interchange of ideas, and a consistent effort of social negotiation to fulfill both individual and collective needs and desires.

*The foundation and the core of
all forms of human social
groups and societies is
communication that is effective
and productive.*

Cooperative and group efforts are impossible to implement without communication, and the success of group efforts is doomed to failure if that communication is not constructive and harmonious.

Effective and productive communication is no less important in today's contemporary world than it was when the predominant human social group on the planet was that of the multi-family band of hunters and gatherers. In fact, it may be even more critical in our modern, 21st-century society because advances in transportation and communication leave all but the most isolated of humans interacting on a daily basis with a diverse set of people.

In the professional world, in the neighborhood and community, and even in our families and social circles, we are far likelier to come into regular contact with people hailing from different nations and cultures, holding a variety of beliefs and cultural orientations, and claiming a different native language, than at any other time in human history.

The Other 55%

When most think of "communication," they think of verbal interactions, of the exchange of spoken words between individuals through the medium of language. And when people study the communication arts, they overwhelmingly tend to focus on the verbal aspect of dialogue. Yet, it has long been known and recognized by anthropologists, psychologists, and other social scientists, discovered and demonstrated through multitudes of formal scientific and behavioral studies, that words and vocabulary play only the smallest part in the overall conveyance of ideas and meaning and offer little to reveal the emotional state of those engaged in communicating.

While the exact percentages are sometimes subject to debate, the most commonly recognized breakdown of how people receive and convey information and understanding through interpersonal communication is that only 7% of it is transmitted through word choices and vocabulary. A more significant 38% comes from tone of voice and the use of tonal inflections, and a whopping 55% are attributed to nonverbal cues, such as facial expressions, body pose and positioning, and other physical gestures and conditions.

Nonverbal signals and cues make up 55% of meanings and messages conveyed and received in interpersonal communication.

That number bears repeating: it is understood and accepted by professionals in fields of psychology, the social sciences, and communication arts that 55% of the information, ideas, and meanings that are conveyed through interpersonal exchange have nothing to do with words and spoken language at all but are instead gleaned from the automatic reading of involuntary nonverbal signals, signs, and cues.

One does not need to be gifted in mathematics to see that this number represents a majority and to grasp the significance and importance of that component of communication. Yet, surprisingly, this aspect of the conveyance and interpretation of information in verbal interactions is generally excluded from the process of language learning and communication studies, both at the early and developmental levels and in contexts of higher education and professional training and development. In spite of being an important—no, a critical—component of human communication, it is rarely addressed in fundamental education.

As such, you should congratulate yourself for taking the initiative and making the effort to fill in this important gap in knowledge by becoming informed about "the other 55%" of human dialogue and exchange. Even if you do not achieve a level of mastery in reading others and learning to control the nonverbal cues that you reveal when communicating with others, you are still sure to benefit from what you can learn in this book.

Not Everything Can Be Controlled

For all of the research that has been conducted around body language, little is still known and understood about the origins and primary basis of the functions of nonverbal communication. In the 19th century, Charles Darwin suggested that these expressions are hard-wired, rooted in and emerging from the time of early mankind, prior to the development of verbal language. His explanation largely remains unchallenged.

The fact that most nonverbal communication in humans is primarily automatic and involuntary—with some of those expressions, such as heart rate, perspiration, pupil dilation, and other muscle responses, being beyond the conscious and deliberate influence of even the most highly trained master of physical self-control—lends credence to the acceptance of these forms of communication as biological adaptations for a social world in which expression via oral language was not an option. The true origin of these nonverbal expressions is not yet fully known and understood, however. Some suggest that the question is irrelevant, that what genuinely matters is understanding how it functions, not its source and origin.

Some involuntary expressions are impossible to control, such as heart rate, perspiration, and pupil dilation and contraction.

Because the overwhelming majority of nonverbal expressions are involuntary and automatic, you should have limited expectations in terms of your own ability to control the signals and signs that you convey to others through your body language. Yet the positive flip side, the advantageous trade-off, is that you can usually expect the cues that you perceive and read in others to be genuine, to offer valuable and accurate information about the thoughts, feelings, and motives of others. Whether not people want to reveal those things is irrelevant; if you know how to read them, the signs will invariably be there.

Context is King

A tremendously important note to offer before getting into the specific details and examples of personality types and nonverbal expressions is that nothing is absolute when it comes to reading people and their nonverbal signals and signs. There is no guaranteed formula for interpreting the unspoken messages that are conveyed through body language. Communication is like a path, a journey, and interactions with every individual in every type of context represents a unique landscape, with its own roads and vistas, its own easily identifiable landmarks and peculiar out-of-the-way dives, that need to be explored and understood in their own particular terms.

Every person possesses an individual set of behaviors, habits, and tendencies, some of which can negate common understandings of nonverbal cues. There are chronically nervous people who seem stressed out even when sitting at home alone, "Type B" people whose heart rates wouldn't increase by a digit even if a deadline for a project was only an hour away, and there are some under the influence of medications that can mask natural responses and make it a challenge to read them. There are a multitude of factors that can skew your results or change the meaning of the nonverbal messages that you are receiving from them.

As such, context is king when embarking on the effort of reading someone's body language. It is of the utmost importance to pay attention to things like personality type, environment, and subtle non-behavioral clues when attempting to assess and interpret someone's nonverbal signals. She might not be tense, she could simply be cold. He might not be lying, he could actually just have a skin rash. They might not be bored, they could be worried about an important impending deadline that you assigned to them.

Communication is also a two-way street. The way that someone conducts his or her self and converses with you is different from the way that he or she would behave with another individual.

Human interaction is just that: interaction. It is an interplay between messages conveyed and received, and when you are in exchange with someone, you are an active participant, not just a passive audience. And the signals and signs that **you** are putting off are unquestionably and unavoidably influencing the signals and signs that your conversational partner is offering to you. You need to be aware of how you may be influencing—even steering—the thrust of the communicational landscape, and take that into account when reading and interpreting another.

Effective body language and personality reading require paying more attention to the other person than to your own thoughts.

Those best-known for their skill in reading people consistently cite one primary rule when trying to interpret body language: pay attention! You have to be more focused on what the other person is communicating than on your own thoughts and agenda if you hope to read that person correctly.

In short, there are no effortless ways to read and interpret body language in individuals and groups. Understanding people and what they are trying to tell you (or trying NOT to tell you) is a process. It involves effort and attention. As mentioned, it is a journey. But like most journeys, there is an eventual payoff in the reaching of the destination. Taking time and putting effort into recognizing and understanding the messages that people are conveying in tandem with, or below the surface of, their spoken works can lead to more fruitful and constructive relationships, a better sense of connection and cooperation, and a greater range of opportunities to reach your personal aims and achieve success.

If Context is King, the Queen is the Cluster

Expression Clusters

Alongside context, recognizing that effective body language reading involves assessing clusters of signals, signs, and cues is of utmost importance. While there are a few single-gesture signals that convey meaning, most involve a collection of expressions and need to be examined as much to be understood. Remember that body language is truly a form of language, and you need to pay attention to its figurative "grammar" and context to accurately interpret it.

Context is king, and expression clusters are queens. Both are required for accurate reading of body language and personality.

Chapter 2 – The Roadmap: Personality

People are complex, and analyzing and understanding them involves observing, assessing, and finding the meaning behind their words and manner of speaking, their nonverbal expressions, their goals and priorities, and what they value and strive to accomplish in interpersonal interactions.

This chapter will teach you how to speed read people by determining personality types and tips for communicating more effectively, once you know someone's type.

Personality Speed Reading

A useful method for reading the meanings behind people's behaviors and facilitating improved communication is through an understanding of their personality types.

The Meyers-Briggs scale of personality types, which is based on the work of psychologist Carl G. Jung, divides people into specific types according to four metrics that are determined by where a person falls on a spectrum of eight opposing tendencies and inclinations in personality. This personality typing has been a well-known and useful measure for pinpointing and understanding behavior and conduct.

Determining one's type on the Meyers-Briggs scale with absolute accuracy requires taking a test. You can make an educated guess at a person's type simply by observation and interaction, though, as many of the personality tendencies have clear external markers.

Personality Type Metrics

The metrics for determining a personality type involve locating a person on a scale for the following diametric opposites:

- Introversion and Extroversion, signified by an I or an E.
- Intuitive or Sensing, signified by an N or an S.
- Thinking or Feeling, signified by a T or an F.
- Judging or Perceiving, signified by a J or a P.

There are 16 different personality types, based upon where a person falls in each of the metrics:

- ISTJ
- ISFJ
- INFJ
- INTJ
- ISTP
- ISFP
- INFP
- INTP
- ESTP
- ESFP
- ENFP
- ENTP
- ESTJ
- ESFJ
- ENFJ
- ENTJ

Extravert and Introvert

This part of a personality involves how a person derives energy and a sense of well-being. Think of every person as having a battery that needs to be charged for him/her to feel good. Extraverts get their batteries charged by interacting with other people and will come away from social activities feeling energetic and enthusiastic. An Introvert's battery gets drained from social interaction, and he/she will need to recharge through solitude and solitary activities. Both types can be equally sociable, but their response to that social activity is different.

Intuitive or Sensing

This part of a personality involves how a person perceives and takes in information about the activities of life and the world. Sensing individuals tend to focus on information that comes from the five senses, the details and tangible factors of a situation, a thing, or a person. Intuitive people tend to process information on a more abstract, creative, "big picture" level. Both types can be detail-oriented and creative, but their overall focus of perception is different.

Thinking or Feeling

This part of a personality involves how a person processes information and approaches decision-making. Thinkers are more comfortable operating on a rational and analytic level, weighing possible outcomes through a logical framework to come to practical decisions. Feeling individuals have more of an empathetic and sensitive approach and will make decisions according to their potential emotional impact.

Both types can be rational and empathetic, but their ultimate preference for the outcome of their decisions is different.

Judging or Perceiving

This part of a personality involves how a person implements knowledge and information, how they apply it to the situations in their lives. Perceiving individuals tend to like to keep things open, to avoid situations that have rigid and constricting parameters, such as projects with deadlines and strict schedules. Judging individuals tend to prefer to have things settled and pinned down, valuing organization and desiring to be in control of a situation. Both types can be organized and abhor a deadline, but their overall tendencies in the types of situations they will be drawn to are different.

Type Markers

As mentioned, absolutely accurate personality typing requires taking a test. Yet as each aspect of personality has a number of external markers, it is possible to make a general estimation of one's personality by observing and interacting with them.

E —Extravert Markers

In social interactions, Extraverts tend to:

- Think out loud
- Talk a lot, talk more, and talk louder
- Use "we" instead of "I"
- Initiate a conversation
- Interrupt a speaker or finish his/her sentences
- Seek to be the center of attention
- Have a difficult time maintaining steady eye contact

Extraverts also prefer to:

- Go places with others, even practical errands
- Enjoy activities and hobbies that involve others
- Choose careers that involve social interaction
- Dress in colorful clothing or flamboyantly

I —Introvert Markers

In social interactions, Introverts tend to:

- Be more comfortable with silence
- Think before speaking or responding

- Talk in a steady, sometimes quiet, tone
- Wait to be approached
- Avoid being the center of attention
- Maintain focus on a speaker through steady eye contact

Introverts also prefer to:

- Go places, particularly tending to practical errands, alone
- Enjoy solitary and quiet activities and hobbies
- Choose careers where social interaction is limited
- Dress in a more subdued or neutral manner

N —Intuitive Markers

In social interactions, Intuitives tend to:

- Have a complex, even unusual, speech pattern
- Jump from one subject to another
- Communicate to express him/her self
- Speak in metaphorical terms
- Repeat and rephrase ideas already stated
- Describe things in a large, big picture sense

Intuitives also prefer to:

- Choose careers that involve creative work
- Pursue graduate-level educations
- Prefer fiction books
- Have more of a future-based attitude, instead of focusing on the past

S —Sensing Markers

In social interactions, Sensors tend to:

- Speak in a clear and straightforward way
- Express linear, sequential thoughts
- Communicate to accomplish something
- Speak in literal terms
- Describe things in a detailed and factual manner
- Tend to be direct, getting to the point

Sensors also:

- Choose careers that involve practical work
- Choose technical or vocational educations
- Read non-fiction books
- Have an accurate recollection of the past

T —Thinking Markers

In social interactions, Thinkers tend to:

- Be aloof and distant
- Speak in a blunt and businesslike manner
- Give an impression of insensitivity
- Appear assertive
- Speak in an impersonal way

Thinkers also prefer to:

- Avoid offering praise or using personal names
- Seek debate and argument for entertainment
- Choose careers that involve strategy
- Plan schedules for others

F —Feeling Markers

In social interactions, Feelers tend to:

- Be warm and friendly
- Speak in a diplomatic and polite way
- Give an impression of sensitivity
- Have difficulty asserting themselves
- Speak in an emotional way

Feelers also prefer to:

- Offer praise and use people's names frequently
- Avoid conflicts and confrontations
- Choose careers in a service industry
- Work around the schedules of others

J —Judging Markers

In social interactions, Judgers tend to:

- Be formal, serious, conventional
- Seek to be in control
- Make quick decisions

Judgers also:

- Keeping a neat appearance
- Are goal driven, enjoying finishing projects
- Appreciate structures and rules
- Are tidy and well-organized
- Walk and move quickly, keep a good posture
- Choose careers where they can have control

P —Perceiving Markers

In social interactions, Perceivers tend to:

- Be casual, playful, unconventional
- Do not mind if others take the lead
- Procrastinate

Perceivers also:

- May appear a bit unkempt
- Are adaptable, prefer starting projects
- Prefer to avoid structures and rules
- Can be messy and disorganized
- Move in a more leisurely pace, have a loose posture
- Choose careers where they can have fun

Personality Group Types

Within the 16 individual types are four categories of group types, based upon combinations of the Intuitive/Sensing and Thinking/Feeling metrics. The first step of speed reading a person is to determine which group type a person falls into, so it is important to become familiar with these clusters of qualities.

Traditionalists – Sensing Judgers (SJ)

- Value organization, structure, rules
- Strive to be reliable, dependable, hard-working
- Usually serious and straightforward
- Respectful, polite, often formal
- Tend to dress conservatively and have a neat appearance
- Move quickly and have good posture
- Direct and efficient communication style
- Focus on tangible matters, not hypotheticals
- Responsible, efficient workers
- Prefer hobbies involving physical activity

Experiencers – Sensing Perceivers (SP)

- Tend to dislike authority and avoid rules and structures
- Have a fun-loving, even playful, attitude
- Are spontaneous and free-spirited
- Possess a curious nature, can be risk-takers or thrill-seekers
- Express an easy-going and relaxed demeanor
- Dress for comfort and have a relaxed dress style

- Speak in an uncomplicated and casual style
- Possess a high level of awareness about their bodies
- Are generally energetic and have strong physical skills of coordination and agility
- Prefer work that involves service, even heroics

Conceptualizers – Intuitive Thinkers (NT)

- Have a strong need for independence
- Frequently overachievers with a tendency to strive for perfection
- Have logical and analytical natures
- Are comfortable with theoretical and abstract ideas
- Give an impression of being overconfident
- Often dress in a way to emphasize either status or independence
- Tend to enjoy language and have a complex speaking style
- Prefer activities with intellectual and theoretical components
- Have strong mechanical and technical skills
- Seek out hobbies that promote self-improvement

Idealists – Intuitive Feelers (NF)

- Highly value integrity
- Have a strong interest in self-knowledge and self-discovery
- Project an empathetic and charismatic demeanor
- Prioritize harmonious relationships and work to cultivate them
- Tend to be idealistic, philosophical, spiritual
- Prefer to speak personal, even intimate, conversational subjects
- Tend to dress in a nonconventional, even rebellious, style
- Can be easily offended by insensitivity and meanness to others
- More imaginative than physical
- Prefer activities that have a positive impact on people, society, and the world

How to Speed Read a Personality

Being familiar with the individual and group types and their qualities and external markers allows for a quick read to determine one's personality type. It is a three-step process, starting with defining a person's group type. By assessing physical demeanor and paying attention to the subjects that one speaks about, it is usually possible to determine one's group type.

Step One: Determine Group Type

Study the different group qualities and practice by asking yourself questions about yourself and the people in your life—can you tell which group they belong to?

You can also practice by asking yourself questions about people you do not know, learning to become more observant to see which group type they are consistent with, such as:
Which seems to describe the person better:

- Dress: Conventional (SJ) or nonconventional (NF), relaxed (SP) or unique (NT)?
- Demeanor: Controlled (SJ) or easy-going (SP), overconfident (NT) or empathetic (NF)?
- Speaking Style: Direct (SJ) or casual (SP), complex (NT) or emotional (NF)?

The more you practice both observing and lining up observations with group types, the easier it will become to get a quick read on which of the four groups a person belongs to.

Step Two: Determine Second-Level Individual Type

After a group type has been determined, figuring out where a person falls a third metric helps is the next step in establishing one's full personality type. For Traditionalists (SJ) and Experiencers (SP), the third metric is Thinking/Feeling, for Conceptualizers (NT) and Idealists (NF), it is the Judging/Perceiving metric.

Cues for determining if Traditionalists (SJ) and Experiencers (SP) have expressed Feeling (F):

- They seek approval, make efforts to connect with and please others
- They tend to be charismatic, charming
- They have an expressive aura

Cues for determining if Traditionalists (SJ) and Experiencers (SP) have expressed Thinking (T):

- They give the impression of being impersonal, disengaged
- They seem to be self-interested
- They tend to be reserved and unemotional

Cues for determining if Conceptualizers (NT) and Idealists (NF) have expressed Perceiving (P):

- They seem gentle and cooperative
- They can be sensitive, even prone to moodiness
- They tend to be humble and embarrassed by praise

Cues for determining if Conceptualizers (NT) and Idealists (NF) have expressed Judging (J):

- They are direct and businesslike
- They can seem brutally honest, even unfeeling
- They are unemotional and physically reserved

Step Three: Determine Full Individual Type

Consider the things that you observed that helped you to determine group and second-level individual type, and review the markers for extraversion or introversion. Chances are that specific characteristics and behaviors were evident, allowing you to make a safe determination of the final piece in the puzzle of the personality type.

Putting it to Work

Once you've determined someone's personality type, you will understand how they think and behave, what they value and prioritize, and the most effective ways to communicate with them.

Helpful hints for communicating with:

Extraverts:

- Keep them verbally engaged
- Allow them the airtime that they need to talk
- Allow the conversation to keep moving
- Expect that they will have an immediate response

Introverts:

- Stick to one subject at a time
- Communicate in written form whenever possible
- Provide time for them to think about something before expecting a response
- Listen to what they say, avoid interrupting

Sensors:

- Offer a clear topic with specific facts and examples
- Provide a step-by-step communication of information
- Emphasize uses and applications that are practical in nature
- Give real-life examples from the past

Intuitives:

- Emphasize on possibilities and the big picture
- Use metaphors and analogies to engage their imaginations
- Brainstorm with them
- Don't present them with too many details

Thinkers:

- Present information in a logical, organized way
- Emphasize cause/effect and consequences
- Avoid repeating yourself
- Request their thoughts on a matter, not their feelings

Feelers

- Start from a place of agreement
- Offer appreciation and recognize their feelings
- Communicate in a friendly and considerate manner
- Emphasize the personal impact of efforts

Judgers

- Communicate in a decisive and solutions-minded way
- Be efficient, organized, and prompt
- Honor previous agreements and plans
- Offer opportunities to make decisions

Perceivers

- Give them space to ask questions and ruminate on a subject
- Allow them the opportunity to provide feedback and modify plans
- Present them with choices and options
- Have an open mind for new ideas and information

Chapter 3 – The Roadmap: Body Language

Nonverbal communication, or kinesics, what we commonly term "body language" is aptly named, as is entails and involves nearly every area of the body. Some signals, signs, and cues can involve only one body part and form of gesture, but in most cases, meaningful forms of nonverbal communication are conveyed through action and activity in multiple parts of the body, in clusters of actions and reaction that, when combined together, translate into a certain meaning.

To create the roadmap to assist in understanding the significance of nonverbal expressions, it is best to explore different areas of the body and the messages that they convey, both alone and in conjunction with other parts of the body in active gestures.

This is far from a dictionary of possible nonverbal expressions. It has been ascertained that the human face alone is capable of making up to 10,000 different expressions, each possessing meaning. Cataloging the full range of body language expressions would be an epic task, and the result might not prove to be particularly enlightening or helpful. Most are more interested in information that proves to be of practical value.

The human face is capable of making 10,000 unique and meaningful expressions.

With that in mind, this overview of nonverbal expressions will focus on those most common, most likely to be encountered in everyday interactions, and those that will offer the most bang-for-the-buck, as the saying goes, in terms of assisting in understanding the meanings and motives behind the motions that people most often make in interpersonal exchange.

Head-to-Toe Body Map

What follows is a head-to-toe list body parts involved in non-verbal communication and information about their common meaning and behavioral significance. This information is structured in the following way:

Area: Action

- **Common:** Most commonly accepted meaning
- **Variant:** Variations in meaning
- **Be Aware:** Conditions or context that could affect
- **Notes:** Any additional information of significance or importance.

Head, Neck, Facial Features

Eyes

One of the most common and well-known idioms about eyes is that they are "the windows to the soul," which suggests that they permit a view into one's internal self. In reading nonverbal signals, signs, and cues, the eyes, along with the hands, are the most valuable resource and reference point in assessing a person's mood, feelings, thoughts, reactions, and intentions. Given how many things can be involuntarily expressed through the eyes, they should be your starting point when reading a person.

Eye Contact

Turning one's eyes to make a visual connection with someone else's eyes, or what we term "eye contact," is a strong nonverbal gesture that serves a variety of functions and reveals much about a person's aims and intentions. It serves as an expression of interest in a conversation or interaction and it signals an ongoing engagement (or lack thereof) in an exchange, as well as provides indicators of the type of relationship that either currently exists or that is desired between the individuals.

Eyes: Pupils and the Limbic System

Where almost all body language is the product of involuntary actions and reactions, the eyes are even more so, with their motions deeply connected to the limbic system, the part of the brain that is involved with emotions, arousal/stimulation, and memories. Certain eye responses, such as pupil dilation and contraction are physiological in nature, possible to influence, but not possible to control.

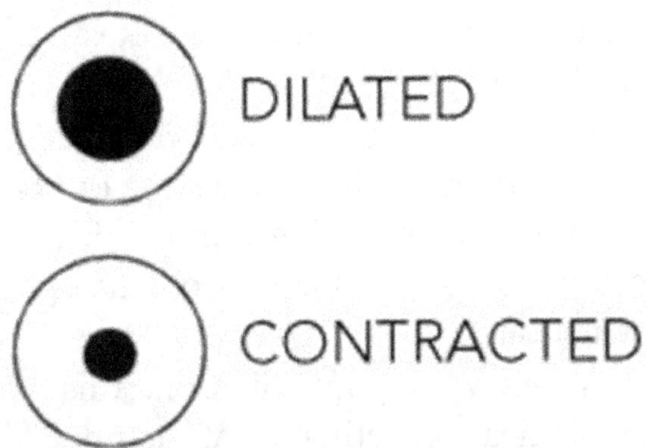

Eyes: Pupils Dilated (Mydriasis)

- **Common:** Attraction, Interest, Arousal.
- **Variant:** In combination with other symbols of stress, can indicate a "Fight or Flight" response.

- **Be Aware:** Pupils also dilate in conditions of low lighting. Dilation also results when an individual has ingested or is under the influence of certain medications and illicit substances.
- **Notes:** This is a physiological response and can be evoked, but not controlled.

Eyes: Pupils Contracted (Miosis).

- **Common:** Lack of interest, Disengagement.
- **Variant:** In combination with signals of relaxation, may suggest a "Rest and Digest" attitude.
- **Be Aware:** Pupils also contract in response to bright light. Ingesting or being under the influence of certain medications and illicit substances can also cause pupil contraction.
- **Notes:** As with pupil dilation, this is a physiological reacting that cannot be controlled without using external means, such as changing the amount of light exposure.

Eyes: Neuro-linguistic Programming

One of the most commonly cited—and misunderstood, therefore controversial—methods of reading the general nature of people's thoughts and motives is through the direction of their involuntary eye movements. Neuro-linguistic Programming (NLP) asserts that automatic directional movements of the eyes indicate the type of thought processes being accessed by the brain. This was long thought to represent a sort of shortcut to determine if someone was lying or engaging in deception, but numerous studies have proven that to be an unfounded claim. You cannot tell if someone is lying simply from the direction in which they turn their eyes when speaking or answering a question.

Movements of the eyes do reliably reveal the type of thought process that someone is experiencing, however, with the types being visual, auditory, kinesthetic, and what is termed "auditory digital" thoughts.

In eye movements, the left side is considered to be attached to memory and recall and the right side to creative and constructed thought processes. Further, looking in an upward direction signifies visual brain activity, looking to the side is recognized as auditory (as in looking towards the ears), and downward looks are self-referencing, involving thoughts about emotions, internal dialogue, and one's sense of physical self.

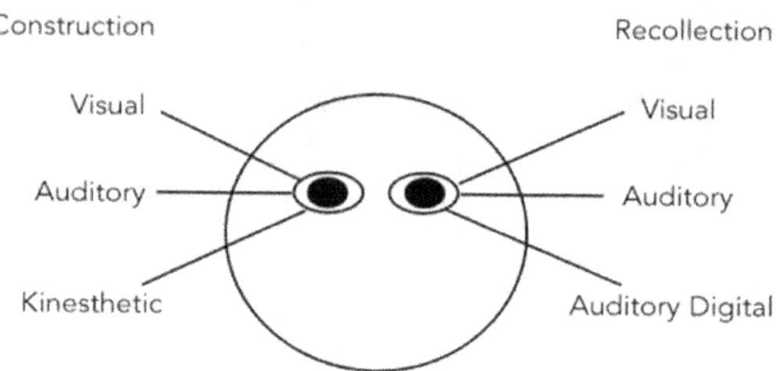

The specific directions and their associated thought processes:

- Up and to the left: Visual recollection and memory.
- Up and to the right: Visual constructed or created thought.
- Sideways to the left: Auditory recollection and memory.
- Sideways to the right: Auditory constructed or created thought.
- Down and the left: Internal conversation and dialogue.
- Down and the right: Internal emotions and sense of one's body.

While some have equated the connection between looking up and to the right with constructed thought and interpreted it as a shortcut to reveal lying, that link has been disproven through formal studies. As such, it is inadvisable to assume that an individual is practicing deception when he/she exhibits that eye movement when speaking or answering a question, particularly if other body language cues indicate openness and sincerity. If it only one part of a cluster of signals signifying deception, however, such as such as covering the mouth with a hand and part of a close arm-cross, cuing tension and self-protection, it could be a good indicator of deception.

Eyes: Opened wide.

- **Common:** Surprise, Excitement.
- **Variant:** In combination with a downturned mouth, can convey disbelief or disapproval.

Eyes: Narrowed.

- **Common:** Suspicion, Distrust, Skepticism.
- **Variant:** In combination with a lowered head, can be a threatening gesture.

Eyes: Downturned.

- **Common:** Disinterest, Discomfort, Avoidance.
- **Variant:** When combined with lowered brows and slumped shoulders, can indicate sorrow and/or feelings of shame.
- **Variant:** In contexts of interaction with someone exhibiting dominant signals, particularly when a power differential is present, turning the eyes down can be a sign of submission or capitulation.
- **Be Aware:** In several countries in the Middle East and Mediterranean area, meanings for both side-to-side and up-and-down head nodding are reversed.
- **Notes:** This is believed to originate in infancy, through turning the head to the side to refuse feeding.

Eyes: Looking sideways.

- **Common:** Uncertainty, Concern.
- **Variant:** Rapid sideways eye motions, or "darting eyes," may indicate fear, an unconscious mimic of looking for an escape route.

Eyes: Frequent blinking.

- **Common:** Disinterest, Boredom.
- **Variant:** Fast, frequent blinking signals fear or being poised to respond to a threat.
- **Variant:** Frequent blinking can be an indicator of a perspective of superiority, particularly when coupled with a head tilting back and/or steepled fingers.
- **Be Aware:** Eye irritation or burning, as well as fatigue, can result in a greater frequency of blinking.

Eyebrows

Eyebrow motions are often associated with nonverbal signals of dominance and submissiveness.

Eyebrows: Both Raised.

- **Common:** Openness, Emphasis, Intensity.
- **Variant:** Combined with different variations in facial expression, can indicate surprise, inquisitiveness, or disbelief.
- **Variant:** Combined with up-and-down head nodding, can be an expression of agreement or assent.

- **Be Aware:** The raising of both eyebrows is generally understood to be a nonverbal signal of submission and sometimes often involuntarily occurs when one is giving commands or trying to make a convincing argument, as if to soften the dominant or aggressive intent of the words.

Eyebrows: One Raised.

- **Common:** Cynicism, Disbelief, Sarcasm. **Notes:** The ability to raise one eyebrow is uncommon. While the percentage of individuals capable of controlling the muscles to elevate one eyebrow without the other is unknown, it is estimated to be as low as 10%. The lowering of one brow is not associated with any particular meaning.

Eyebrows: Both Lowered.

- **Common:** Annoyance, Anger, Aggression.
- **Variant:** Combined with a downturned mouth and sorrowful facial expression, may suggest sadness or depression.

- **Variant:** Combined with a lower head, can indicate a desire to deceive or conceal intentions.
- **Be Aware:** The lowering of both eyebrows is generally understood to be a nonverbal signal of dominance and can be interpreted as an aggressive gesture, evoking a response of defensiveness.

Eyes: Tips

Pay attention to the movement of one's eyes when they are speaking. Remember, the left is memory; the right is constructed or created thought.

A rapid raising and lowering of both eyebrows, or what is called an "eyebrow flash," may be intended to indicate romantic interest, but is usually perceived as lecherous.

To soften the dominant or aggressive intent of commands, orders, or emphatic arguments, be careful to keep your eyebrows in a neutral or raised position.

To convey superiority, tilt your head back while holding your hands together with steepled fingers and blink at a more frequent rate than usual.

Mouth

While the mouth may seem like a reliable indicator of mood and one's feelings, the lower half of the face is easier to control than the upper half, and not all mouth expressions may be genuine. It is advisable to look at the eyes and other body language cues to determine the accuracy of a person's mouth signals

Mouth: Both Corners Turned Up (Grin, Smile).

- **Common:** Positive, Happiness, Contentment.
- **Variant:** If other signals of fear or anxiety are present, may indicate fearfulness or stress.

Mouth: One Corner Turned Up (Half-Smile).

- **Common:** Uncertainty, Doubtfulness.
- **Variant:** May indicate sarcasm.
- **Be Aware:** A half-smile is a common feature of the microexpressions of disgust and contempt (see below). If a brief grimace is evident before someone fully smiles, it may not be a genuine expression.

Mouth: Both Corners Turned Down (Frown).

- **Common:** Negative, Dislike, Disapproval.
- **Variant:** If combined with a pouting lower lip, typically an indication of sorrow or sadness.

Mouth: Lips Compressed or Pursed.

- **Common:** Frustration, Disagreement, Controlled Emotion.
- **Variant:** May also signify fear or anger, in combination with other expressions.
- **Be Aware:** This expression may also be part of microexpressions of disgust and contempt (see below).

Mouth: Tip

Remember that the lower half of the face is easier to consciously control. Take a measure of all other nonverbal signals to determine someone's mood, feelings, and response.

Facial Microexpressions – Emotional Indicators

These are clusters of facial expressions, called microexpressions that indicate particular emotions or responses. Seven microexpressions are recognized as universal: happiness, surprise, fear, anger, sadness, disgust, and contempt. Many of the features of the latter two are similar. Stress and anxiety also feature as a cluster of facial expression.

Microexpressions occur very rapidly, passing over a face as quickly as $1/15^{th}$ to $1/25^{th}$ of a second. As such, they are difficult to capture in motion. An observant body language may be able to spot the expression and get a quick speed read on someone's feelings and response.

Happiness, Pleasure:

- Fine wrinkles at the outside edges of the eyes (crow's feet)
- Raised cheeks
- Visible line from the bottom of the nose to edge of lips (laugh lines)
- Corners of mouth are turned upward (smile)

Surprise:

- Raised eyebrows, wrinkling forehead
- Eyes opened wide, whites of the eyes clearly visible
- Open mouth, parted teeth, slack mouth expression

Fear:

- Eyebrows drawn together, creating a straight horizontal line
- Wrinkling between the eyebrows and vertically up the forehead
- Tense and slightly open mouth

Anger:

- Bunching and drawing together of the eyebrows, may create a vertical line
- Expression may stare or bulge
- Tightly pursed lips, mouth downturned
- Jutting of the lower jaw

Sadness, Sorrow:

- Bunching and drawing up of the eyebrows, triangulated
- Corners of the mouth are downturned
- Pouting of the lower lip

Disgust, Contempt:

- Squinting eyes
- Long periods of eyes being closed in blinking, or eyelid flutter (indicates strong disagreement)
- Eye rolling
- Raised upper eyelids
- Raised cheeks
- Wrinkling of the nose (disgust)
- Mouth in a cynical half-smile (contempt)
- Lips pursed

Nervousness, Anxiety:

- Forehead furrowed
- Eyes squinting
- Lips pursed or drawn into the mouth
- Quivering in the lower face, lips, and chin
- Twitching mouth

Extreme Stress, Tension:

Note: These expressions can develop into permanent ticks.

- Rapid blinking
- Twitching cheeks and/or eyes
- Thrusting forward or sideways movement of the jaw
- Biting the tongue or inside of the cheeks
- Nervous touching of the eyelids, nose, or ends of hair

Head

There are a number of meaning-laden gestures and nonverbal communication signals that involve a combination of the head and the hand(s). Those gestures are listed and described in the "Hands" section later in this book.

Head: Nodding side-to-side.

- **Common:** No, Negative, Refusal.
- **Variant:** In combination with certain facial expressions, can signal disbelief or uncertainty.
- **Be Aware:** In several countries in the Middle East and Mediterranean area, meanings for both side-to-side and up-and-down head nodding are reversed.
- **Notes:** This is believed to originate in infancy, through turning the head to the side to refuse feeding.

Head: Nodding up-and-down.

- **Common:** Yes, Affirmative, Agreement, Approval, Understanding.
- **Variant:** Slow nodding is a signal of interest. Rapid nodding indicates impatience or lack of interest. Forceful nodding typically accompanies strong, emphatic feelings.
- **Be Aware:** Men and women use and interpret head nodding in a conversation in different ways. For men, it signifies agreement; for women, it signifies interest and a desire to continue the conversation.
- **Be Aware:** Certain medical conditions cause involuntary tremors of the head, resembling gestural nods. If someone appears to have tremors in other parts of the body, or if his/her nodding seems either unusual or excessive, it may be the result of such a condition.

Head: Tilted to the side.

- **Common:** Interest, Responsive, Engaged.
- **Variant:** In romantic contexts, a head tilted to the side can indicate coyness.

Head: Tilted backward.

- **Common:** Uncertainty, Suspicion.
- **Variant:** In combination with raised eyebrows, a head tilted backward can indicate arrogance, disdain, or a feeling of superiority over the conversational partner(s).

Head: Tips

The meanings of up-and-down and side-to-side head nodding vary in the Middle East and the Mediterranean. Be careful to be aware of the differences when you are traveling.

Men and women use and interpret head nodding differently. For men, it means they are in agreement; for women, it means they are interested in and want to continue the conversation.

To show romantic interest, tilt your head to one side while looking at or listening to the object of your interest.

Neck/Throat

Most body language gestures that involve the

neck and throat also involve the hand(s). Those gestures are listed and described in the "Hands" section later in this book.

Throat: Hard swallowing.

- **Common:** Embarrassed, Anxious, Stressed.
- **Variant:** Rapid swallowing can signify fear.
- **Be Aware:** Rapid and/or hard swallowing can be a response to a sore throat or other illness that affects saliva production. Look for other signs that the individual might be unwell before assuming the meaning of the gesture.

Throat: Clearing while speaking.

- **Common:** Uncertainty, Feeling Self-Conscious.
- **Variant:** Excessive or noticeably unusual throat clearing while speaking can indicate deception and dishonesty.
- **Be Aware:** Throat clearing can be associated with a cough or other illness that irritates the throat. Cigarette smokers may also engage in more throat clearing. Look for signs to determine if the

individual might be unwell, or a smoker, before interpreting the meaning of the gesture.

Throat: Clearing while listening.

- **Common:** Anxiety, disagreement, doubt.
- **Variant:** A forceful or aggressive clearing of the throat can be used to interrupt or challenge a speaker, or to draw attention to one's self.
- **Be Aware:** As with other swallowing and clearing signals, this may be an indication of illness or some other physical issue. Use caution in using only this signal to interpret motives and meanings.

Throat: Jumping Adam's Apple.

- **Common:** Anxiety, Nervousness, Stress, Embarrassment.
- **Be Aware:** This is a nonverbal expression exclusive to males, due to physiology.

Throat: Tip

If someone clears their throat excessively or in a noticeably unusual way, that's an indicator of deception and dishonesty.

Shoulders, Arms, Hands

The upper part of the body provides a wealth of information in body language reading. Shoulders are recognized as being controlled by muscles that are sensitive to emotions, and hands, along with eyes and facial features are one of the surest indicators of a person's thoughts, feelings, and reactions.

Shoulders

Shoulders: Shrug/Shrugging.

- **Common:** Uncertainty, Insecure.
- **Variant:** A shrug sustained in a raised position can indicate defensiveness or extreme tension.
- **Be Aware:** When a shrug seems to contradict spoken words, it can be an indication of an attempt to mislead or be deliberately ambiguous.
- **Notes:** This is believed to originate in infancy, through turning the head to the side to refuse feeding.

Shoulders: Squared, Pushed Back.

- **Common:** Asserting dominance.
- **Variant:** May be an indicator that someone is poised for a confrontation.
- **Notes:** Squared shoulders are associated with masculinity and strength.

Shoulders: Slumping.

- **Common:** Resignation, Dejection, Depression.
- **Variant:** Slumping shoulders may indicate the submission to a dominant expression in another in order to avoid conflict and confrontation.

Shoulders: Rotating.

- **Common:** Aggression, if not done within the context of preparing for exercise.
- **Variant:** If done while another is speaking, an indicator of dismissal and disregard of what is being said. Can be a clear indicator of an intention to be disrespectful.

Shoulders: Tips

When a shrug contradicts spoken words, it can be an indication of an attempt to mislead or be ambiguous.

Rotating your shoulders while someone is speaking is a signal of disrespect.

To avoid conflict and confrontation with someone exhibiting aggressive or dominant signals, slump your shoulders to signify submission.

Arms

Arms: Crossed on Chest.

- **Common:** Defensiveness, Self-Protection, Insecurity.
- **Variant:** Multiple. The height of the arms and hands, and the placement and form of the hands, all have variants in meaning (see below).
- **Be Aware:** Arm crossing is a universally recognized negative gesture, which serves to decrease an impression of credibility. Even if it feels comfortable, it should be avoided in contexts where one is attempting to establish or maintain credibility.

Arms: Crossed on Chest, Torso Leaning Back.

- **Common:** Dominant, Defensiveness.
- **Be Aware:** This is a gesture of dominance, accompanying defensiveness. If combined with facial expressions of contempt, it can be interpreted as haughtiness or cockiness.

Arms: Crossed on Chest, Hands Clenched in Fists.

- **Common:** Hostile Defensiveness.
- **Be Aware:** This gesture indicates aggression and a readiness to attack, particularly if it is combined with facial expressions revealing anger, disgust, or contempt.

Arms: Crossed on Chest, Hands Gripping Arms.

- **Common:** Fearful Defensiveness.
- **Be Aware:** This gesture is a form of self-soothing, a self-hug, to protect and reinforce in situations that are threatening or fearful (i.e. before a plane flight, in a doctor's office)

Arms: Crossed on Chest, Upward Pointing Thumbs.

- **Common:** Superiority, Defensiveness.
- **Be Aware:** This gesture reveals an attitude of superiority, along with a defensiveness, and is reinforced when the person holding this position is also rocking on the balls of the feet. It may be used in response to a dominant expression in another.

Arms: One Arm Crossed on Chest, Holding Other Upper Arm.

- **Common:** Insecurity, Self-Protection.
- **Be Aware:** This gesture, most frequently seen in women, suggests lack of confidence or unease in social situations.

Arms: Arms in a Downward V, Hands Together.

- **Common:** Insecurity, Self-Protection.
- **Be Aware:** This gesture, most frequently seen in men, suggests lack of confidence or unease in social situations. It visually appears that the person is protecting his groin area.

Arms: Arms Behind Back, Hands Together.

- **Common:** Confidence, Fearlessness.
- **Be Aware:** This gesture, which opens the body, can be interpreted as a signal of superiority or dominance, if other such cues are present.

Arms: Arms Behind Back, One Hand Gripping an Arm or Wrist.

- **Common:** Frustration, Anger.
- **Be Aware:** This gesture is associated with an effort to maintain self-control. If there are cues indicating anger, a confrontation may be possible.

Arms: Tips

Crossed arms decrease an impression of credibility. Even if it's comfortable, avoid it in contexts where you are trying to establish or maintain credibility.

Leaning back while your arms are crossed conveys cockiness and haughtiness.

Some women express lack of confidence or unease in social situations by crossing one arm over their body and gripping the other arm, forming a sort of barrier.

If one arm is crossed behind someone's back, in the same way, it means that someone is trying to maintain self-control. If signs of anger are present, watch out for a confrontation!

Pointing your thumbs upward while crossing your chest signifies an attitude of superiority, along with defensiveness.

Hands

Hands are one of the most expressive parts of the body, along with eyes and facial expressions. How they are held and what actions they perform are very reliable components of accurately reading body language.

Hands: Both Palms Facing Up.

- **Common:** Openness, trustworthiness.
- **Variant:** If combined with a shrug or certain facial expressions, can indicate uncertainty.

Hands: One or Both Palms Facing Down.

- **Common:** Dominance, Authority, Expression of Power.

- **Be Aware:** This gesture has a strong connection to the historical period when Germany was under Nazi control and, if used, may be interpreted as a deliberate attempt to associate with such.

Hands: Palms Rubbing Together.

- **Common:** Positive, Anticipation, Expectation.
- **Be Aware:** This is also a gesture associated with the warming of one's hands. Be careful to check for other positive expressions or for signs that the individual might be cold before assuming accuracy.

Hands: Clenched.

- **Common:** Negative, Anxious, Tense.
- **Variant:** Hand clenched into fists may also be an indicator or anger.

Hands: Pressed Together Upright (Steepled).

- **Common:** Confidence, Self-Assured, Superiority.
- **Be Aware:** This is also a gesture of

dominance, and expression of superiority, particularly when combined with raised eyebrows and a head tilting back. If combined with facial expressions of contempt, it can be interpreted as haughtiness or cockiness.

Hand and Face Combinations

Nearly all gestures of face touching commonly signify deceit, dishonesty, or an attempt to suppress the truth. These signals are even stronger indicators if more than one of them occurs when discussing the same topic.

Hand: Covering the Mouth.

- **Common:** Suppression, Deceit.
- **Be Aware:** Whether it is the full hand, a fist, or several fingers, this is a signal of suppression of deceitful or dishonest words.

Hand: One Finger Covering the Mouth.

- **Common:** "Be Quiet."
- **Variant:** Tapping one finger on the lips can indicate that someone is thinking or considering something.

Hand: Touching the Nose.

- **Common:** Suppression, Deceit.
- **Variant:** Rubbing one side of the nose can be an indication of disagreement.
- **Variant:** A signal of negative or frustrated evaluation or judgment is the pinching of the bridge of the nose.
- **Variant:** Pressing on the nose is a common cue that someone is thinking or considering something.
- **Be Aware:** Nose touching may be associated with illness, allergies, sinus or skin irritation. Pay attention to the person's overall health and for other signals of unwellness before determining the accuracy of this gesture.

Hand: Touching or Rubbing the Eyes.

- **Common:** Suppression, Deceit.
- **Variant:** Combined with an avoided gaze, this is a clear signal of dishonesty and deceit.
- **Be Aware:** Eye rubbing touching may be associated with eye irritation or fatigue. Pay attention to other signals before determining the accuracy of this gesture.

- **Note:** There is a variation in how men and women exhibit this gesture. Men tend to rub vigorously, while women rub more slowly.

Hand: Stroking the Chin.

- **Common:** Consideration, Decision-Making.
- **Variant:** In a man with a beard, this gesture may be one of self-grooming.

Hand: Pulling an Ear.

- **Common:** Anxiety, Uncertainty.
- **Variant:** This gesture may be an indicator of dishonesty, if found in combination with other signals consistent with deceit.

Hand and Face: Tip

Most self-touching involving the hands and the face signify deceit and dishonesty, especially if they occur in clusters.

Hand and Head Combinations

Hand: Scratching the Neck.

- **Common:** Doubt, Disagreement.
- **Variant:** If the scratching occurs five times and is located right below an ear, it is a commonly understood signal of deceit and dishonesty.

Hand: Open Palm Rubbing the Neck.

- **Common:** Uncertainty, Frustration, Disagreement.
- **Variant:** The closer to the back of the neck the rubbing occurs, the greater the conflict and negative emotion.

Hand: Holding the Head.

- **Common:** Evaluation, Consideration.
- **Variant:** If the chin is resting directly on the palm, this is a body language signal of boredom.

Hand: Joined Behind Head.

- **Common:** Confident, Superiority, Power.
- **Variant:** If the chin is resting directly on the palm, this is a body language signal of boredom.

- **Be Aware:** This a dominance gesture, whether exhibited sitting or standing.
- **Note:** Studies have shown that taking this posture will assist in increasing feelings of confidence and authority.

Hand and Head: Tip

Holding joined hands behind your head while sitting or standing increases feelings of confidence and authority.

Scratching five times below an ear is a cue of dishonesty and deceit.

If your audience is resting their chins on their palms, they're bored!

Hand and Body Combinations

Hand: Resting on Hips.

- **Common:** Preparation, Gearing Up.
- **Variant:** If thumbs are pointing backward, can be a signal of aggression.
- **Variant:** If thumbs are pointing forward, is a cue for thoughtfulness or uncertainty.
- **Be Aware:** If combined with facial expressions of anger, can signify a loss of temper.

Hand and Object Combinations

Hand: Adjusting Cufflinks.

- **Common:** Self-Soothing, Calming of Insecurity.
- **Note:** This is an exclusively masculine gesture.

Hand: Pulling at a Collar.

- **Common:** Frustration, Agitation.
- **Variant:** If combined with other cues of deceit, this may be a cue of dishonesty.

Hand: Fingers Drumming on a Table.

- **Common:** Impatience.
- **Variant:** May be part of a cluster of signals to indicate boredom.

Hand and Body: Tip

The way thumbs are pointed when someone is holding their hands on their hips signals their feelings: pointing forward indicates thoughtfulness or uncertainty, pointing backward can be a signal of aggression or intended confrontation.

Legs, Feet

Legs, Standing and Sitting Positions

At Attention: Legs Together, Upright Posture.

- **Common:** Neutral.
- **Note:** More common in women than men.

Legs Apart: Legs Separated, Upright Posture.

- **Common:** Dominance, Confidence.
- **Note:** More common in men than women.

One Foot Out: One Foot Pointed Ahead, the Other Turned at an Angle

- **Common:** Posing, Attention-Seeking.
- **Note:** The direction in which the pointed foot is turned can give indications of someone's desires or intentions (i.e. towards an exit or an attractive person).

Legs Crossed: Legs Crossed, Upright Posture

- **Common:** Uncertainty, Insecurity.
- **Note:** If accompanied by arms crossed over the chest, defensive or anxious.

Common Sitting Positions

Legs Crossed: At the Knee.

- **Common:** Neutral.
- **Note:** If accompanied by arms crossed over the chest, may indicate disinterest or withdrawal of engagement from a conversation.

Legs Crossed: At the Thigh, Shins Parallel.

- **Common:** Neutral.
- **Note:** Due to bone structure, men cannot sit in this position. It is an exclusively feminine expression that indicates youthfulness and health and is favored by most men.

Legs Crossed: One Shin Resting on Thigh of Other Leg.

- **Common:** Competitive, Argumentative.
- **Note:** Almost exclusively a man gesture, as it represents a "genital display."
- **Note:** This position is interpreted as an insult in some cultures because it shows the bottom of the shoe.

Legs Crossed: On Ankle Resting on Thigh of Other Leg.

- **Common:** Stubborn, Inflexible.
- **Note:** Almost exclusively a man gesture, as it represents a "genital display."
- **Note:** This position is interpreted as an insult in some cultures because it shows the bottom of the shoe.

Legs Crossed: At the Ankle.

- **Common:** Shyness, Withholding Information.
- **Note:** It is important to pay attention to dress when women exhibit this expression, as it may be the product of modesty and not a signal that information is being withheld.

Legs Crossed: Intertwined.

- **Common:** Shyness.
- **Note:** This is an almost exclusively feminine position.

Feet

While there are no real expressions that feet make, they do convey meaning and interests, as feet will involuntarily point towards desired objects and people and point away from people and things that are disliked or that they would prefer to avoid. This is true while an individual is both sitting and standing.

Understand the context and possible variations in meaning, via expression clusters, to fully grasp the nonverbal messages that people are conveying.

Legs and Feet Tips:

People involuntarily point towards desired objects and people and point away from people and things that are disliked or that they would prefer to avoid

Crossing legs with the ankle or shin resting on the other thigh indicate that someone is stubborn, perhaps argumentative. This type of position is known as a "genital display."

Open & Closed Postures

Certain postures convey an impression of either openness or closed guardedness. Those that are closed visually appear to be so, with the crossing of arms and legs, sometimes even with a slumping of shoulders and a downturned head, as if all parts are working together to protect or hide the body. Similarly, open postures also have a visual appearance of openness, with arms at the sides or extended slightly away from the body, legs either straight or slightly separated, shoulders and head upright.

- Closed postures give an impression of uncertainty, defensiveness, weakness, and lack of credibility.
- Open postures convey confidence, authority, strength, and competence.

Your Mom was right—good posture matters!

Quick Read Guide

Remember that most context and clusters need to be considered and examined in order to accurately read a person's nonverbal expressions. Here is a quick summary of some of the expressions that signal certain moods, emotions, or responses.

Signals that indicate Agreement, Approval, Happiness:

- Mouth: Both Corners Turned Up (Grin, Smile).
- Head: Nodding up-and-down.
- Eyebrows: Both Raised. And nodding

Signals that indicate Aggression:

- Eyebrows: Both Lowered.
- Shoulders: Squared, Pushed Back.
- Shoulders: Rotating.
- Arms: Crossed on Chest, Hands Clenched in Fists.
- Hand: Resting on Hips.
- Legs Crossed: One Ankle or Shin Resting on Thigh of Other Leg.

Signals that indicate Anger:

- Eyebrows: Both Lowered.
- Mouth: Lips Compressed.
- Mouth: Lips Pursed.
- Arms: Arms Behind Back, One Hand Gripping an Arm or Wrist.

Signals that indicate Anxiety, Stress:

- Throat: Hard swallowing.
- Throat: Clearing while speaking.
- Hands: Clenched.
- Hand: Pulling an Ear.
- Throat: Jumping Adam's Apple.

Signals that indicate Boredom:

- Eyes: Frequent blinking.
- Hand: Holding the Head.
- Hand: Fingers Drumming on a Table.

Signals that indicate Cynicism, Sarcasm:

- Eyebrows: One Raised.
- Mouth: One Corner Turned Up (Half-Smile).

Signals that indicate Deceit, Dishonesty:

- Eyebrows: Both Lowered. Lowered head
- Hand: Covering the Mouth.
- Hand: Touching the Nose.
- Hand: Touching or Rubbing the Eyes.
- Hand: Pulling an Ear.
- Hand: Scratching the Neck.
- Legs Crossed: At the Ankle. (secrecy)

Signals that indicate Defensiveness:

- Arms: Crossed on Chest.
- Shoulders: Shrug/Shrugging. (held)

Signals that indicate Dislike, Distrust:

- Eyes: Narrowed.
- Mouth: Both Corners Turned Down (Frown).

Signals that indicate Disagreement:

- Mouth: Lips Pursed.
- Head: Nodding side-to-side.
- Throat: Clearing while speaking.
- Hand: Scratching the Neck.
- Hand: Open Palm Rubbing the Neck.

Signals that indicate Disinterest, Discomfort:

- Eyes: Downturned.
- Eyes: Frequent blinking.

Signals that indicate Fear:

- Eyes: Looking sideways.
- Eyes: Frequent blinking.
- Mouth: Lips Compressed or Pursed
- Arms: Crossed on Chest, Hands Gripping Arms. (Defensive)
- Throat: Hard swallowing.

Signals that indicate Frustration:

- Mouth: Lips Compressed.
- Mouth: Lips Pursed.
- Arms: Arms Behind Back, One Hand Gripping an Arm or Wrist.
- Hand: Pulling at a Collar.

Signal and cues that indicate Impatience:

- Hand: Fingers Drumming on a Table.
- Head: Nodding up-and-down. (rapid)

Signals that indicate Interest:

- Eye flash
- Head: Nodding up-and-down.
- Head: Tilted to the side.
- One Foot Out: One Foot Pointed Ahead, the Other Turned at an Angle.

Signals that indicate Sorrow, Depression:

- Eyes: Downturned.
- Eyebrows: Both Lowered. With frown
- Shoulders: Slumping.

Signals that indicate Uncertainty, Insecurity:

- Eyes: Looking sideways.
- Mouth: One Corner Turned Up (Half-Smile).
- Head: Tilted backward.
- Throat: Clearing while speaking.
- Shoulders: Shrug/Shrugging.
- Arms: One Arm Crossed on Chest, Holding Other Upper Arm.
- Arms: Arms in a Downward V, Hands Together.
- Hand: Open Palm Rubbing the Neck.
- Hand: Resting on Hips.
- Legs Crossed: Legs Crossed, Upright Posture.
- Throat: Jumping Adam's Apple.

Dominance and Submission

Certain gestures convey attitudes of dominance and submission.

Signals of Dominance

- Eyes: Frequent blinking.
- Eyebrows: Both Lowered.

- Shoulders: Squared, Pushed Back.
- Arms: Crossed on Chest, Torso Leaning Back.
- Arms: Arms Behind Back, Hands Together.
- Hands: One or Both Palms Facing Down.
- Hands: Pressed Together Upright (Steepled).
- Hand: Joined Behind Head.
- Legs Apart: Legs Separated, Upright Posture.

Signals of Submission

- Eyes: Downturned.
- Eyebrows: Both Raised.
- Shoulders: Slumping.

Chapter 4 – Navigation: Genders

Men and women share a great many nonverbal expressions, but there are some variations in meaning and intentions when conveying and interpreting a number of signals, signs, and cues to thoughts and feelings. This is consistent with all forms of communication, both oral language and body language. Knowing and understanding those variations is a form of examining the context, and one's gender should be considered when reading people.

It is important to note that gender is different from sex, with the latter referring to the physical biology of the body and the former consisting of a set of patterns of behavior and conduct. Unsurprisingly then, communication styles fall along gender lines, not sex, and those who identify with a certain gender share those expressions, regardless of their sex.

Communication styles fall along gender lines, and those who identify with a certain gender share those expressions, regardless of their sex.

A further important note is that dominant and submissive communication expressions tend to fall along gender lines, with the former regarded as predominantly masculine and the latter, feminine. Whether this is the result of ancient biological hard-wiring or cultural influence is uncertain; most experts in the field consider it to be a mix of the two.

This gender-aligned dominance/submissiveness dichotomy in involuntary expressions can be particularly tricky to navigate in the professional arena, as females can be in dominant roles of power and authority just as frequently as males can. Special care should be taken when assessing context in inter-gender communications in the workplace to avoid unnecessary conflict and unintended insubordination.

Gender-Specific Standing and Sitting Positions

Males:

- Males are more likely to stand in an upright posture with legs separated and with arms in a downward V, hands clasped together to shield or protect the groin area.

- Males are more likely to adopt a sitting leg-crossing position with a shin or ankle resting on the thigh of the other leg. Male biology makes sitting with legs crossed at the thigh and shins parallel physically impossible or prohibitively uncomfortable.

Females:

- Females are more likely to stand in an upright posture with legs together and will engage a half-arm-cross stance, with one arm crossing the chest and gripping the other arm.
- Females are more likely to sit with legs crossed at the ankle or with intertwined legs, and they are capable of sitting with legs crossed at the thigh and shins parallel.

Head Nodding

The body language expression of head nodding in an up-and-down motion is one of the greatest sources of misunderstanding between males and females. Males nod to indicate agreement or assent, while females nod as a form of encouragement, indicating her interest in continuing the dialogue. Both males and females need to be aware of this difference to ensure that they are not conveying or interpreting the wrong meaning.

Males nod to indicate agreement or assent, while females nod as a form of encouragement, indicating her interest in continuing the dialogue.

Deceit and Dishonesty

It is understood that males and females have different motivations for lying and deception. Males are more likely to lie about themselves than about others—it is estimated 8 times as likely—and they lie to improve the impression that others have of them, to appear more successful or powerful. Females more often lie to protect others, to spare the feelings of others, or to boost them up or feel better about themselves.

It is also believed that females tend to construct complicated and detailed lies, while men keep it simple when they lie. Yet be warned, it has been demonstrated that females are more adept at picking up signals of deceit—and the reading of nonverbal cues altogether—which is attributed to the more involved role that they typically have with infants in the pre-language stage. Brain studies using Magnetic Resonance Imaging (MRI) reveal that when evaluating and assessing other people, 14-16 areas of the brain are active, while in men, only 4-6 brain areas are engaged when assessing others. When combined with a high Emotional Intelligence level and statistically speaking, a woman is more likely to perceive unspoken and hidden messages than a man.

Females are more adept at picking up signals of deceit. MRI brain studies reveal that 14-16 areas of the female brain are active when evaluating and assessing other people, while only 4-6 brain areas are engaged when males are assessing others.

Most nonverbal signals of deceit or lying are the same between genders, but in males, the rubbing of the eyes is done in a more forceful manner, while females will rub more slowly and delicately. To detect lying in anyone, it is best to consult the full range of expressions that indicate dishonesty and deceit.

Interest and Attraction

There are a number of variations in ways that males and females reveal attraction and interest through nonverbal signals, signs, and cues.

While both genders will convey an attitude of openness, in males, that openness often involves what is termed "genital displays." Males will open the legs, either seated or standing, and will often place their hands in a position to frame the groin area, often by resting fingers in pockets and allowing thumbs to protrude upwards. Conversely, females will keep their arms at their sides and may even straighten in posture to emphasize their breasts, as well as are likely to engage their hands in gestures of self-touching or self-grooming, intended to draw attention to certain feminine features. They will also lean forward, towards the object of attraction. In both genders, feet will involuntarily point towards people and objects they find attractive and interesting.

One notable and nearly exaggerated expression that females will reveal occurs while sitting, in the position of resting the face on the back of the hand, as if presenting her face on a platter. Another is that of lowering the head while keeping the eyes upturned, an exaggerated position of submissiveness.

Pupil dilation when looking at something of interest is common to both genders, as is prolonged eye contact. Context is important when reading these eye signals, however, like low lighting or a general friendly interest can influence and affect both.

The Big Picture

Both males and females have unique personalities and a full range of habits and behaviors that are informed by their upbringing, personal values, professional position, and current aims and goals. The nonverbal cues indicated by body language are only one piece of the puzzle when determining interests, reactions, and motives.

Truly understanding someone requires a combination of a reading of his/her personality and an analysis of all of the messages that they convey in both oral and body language.

Chapter 5 – Navigation: The Workplace

Power Differentials

One of—if not **the**—most important fundamental components in successfully navigating the professional world and workplace is the understanding power differentials, situations in which individuals hold positions with different levels of authority and power, which not only influence but determine, the type of behaviors and conduct expected when those individuals interact with one another.

Whereas social relationships are largely lateral in nature, with everyone relatively equal to each other, there is a hierarchy in the workplace that informs the ways in which people should interact with one another. In many companies and organizations, this hierarchy is not only understood as a concept but also as a structure, sometimes visually expressed as an organizational chart. An organizational chart looks like a pyramid, with those holding the positions of most power and authority at the top, with ever-widening branches of those who are in increasingly lower positions.

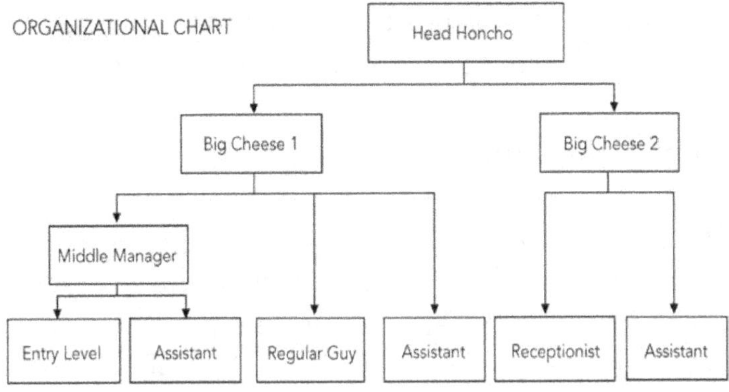

Even though one's position in the hierarchy does not equate to someone being better or worse, or genuinely "superior" or "inferior," the common language in the professional domain refers to those in positions with greater authority as being "higher-ups" or "superiors," and those falling below them on the chart as "subordinates." Those at the same level are usually called co-workers, or lateral co-workers or colleagues, though everyone you work with can be accurately referred to as a colleague.

For the most success in a professional environment, it is important to understand the hierarchy in your company or organization. If an organizational chart does not exist, it could be helpful to create one of your own, to visually understand the structure of authority and where your supervisor(s), colleagues, and your own position falls in that structure, as the way you communicate with those individuals should be informed by those positions.

Professionalism

Individuals are expected to speak, carry themselves, and even often appear and dress in a more formal manner when in the workplace. That code of professional conduct also carries over into communication, including body language. Certain expressions that would be acceptable in other contexts are either not appropriate for the workplace or, if exhibited, can undermine one's opportunities for success and advancement or his/her authority and ability to supervise subordinates effectively.

While there is an expectation (one would hope, anyway) of respectful conduct between individuals at all levels, it is generally accepted—even demanded—that the highest possible level of respect should be given to those who hold positions of more authority and power. There is often even an expectation of deference, of those lower in the hierarchy to defer to those in higher positions via not challenging the wants, orders, and ideas of a superior—or being very cautious when offering a challenge.

Deference and careful, professional communication with those "higher up" is not only helpful in ensuring a working environment without conflict, but it is also typically necessary for those looking to gain recognition and advancement.

There is a fine balance, however, one needs to take a deferential and respectful position and attitude of communication, but also needs to convey confidence and competence. It can be a tricky balancing act, both asserting yourself as a confident and capable worker, without that act of self-assertion threatening the authority of the person/people in the higher position. As such, being aware of nonverbal expressions associated with dominance and submissiveness and making an effort to avoid either displaying or responding to them incorrectly can prevent power struggles and the negative consequences of them.

Asserting yourself as a confident and capable worker, without that act of self-assertion threatening the authority of people in higher positions can be a tricky balancing act.

Signals of Dominance

- Frequent blinking of the eyes and raised eyebrows while someone is speaking.
- Lowered eyebrows while the head is upright
  - Note: Lowered eyebrows and head can be interpreted as an aggressive or confrontational gesture.
- Shoulders squared or pushed back.
- Open stance, legs together, slightly apart, or separated.
- Open stance with arms held behind the back, hands together.
- Hands pressed together upright (Steepled).
- Hands joined together behind the head, an even more powerful if also leaning torso back.
- Legs Crossed with ankle or shin resting on the thigh of the other Leg.
  - Note: Can be interpreted as aggressive, should be used with caution.

Signals of Submission

- Downturned eyes.
- Raised eyebrows with an open facial expression.
- Slumping shoulders.
- Closed body posture.
- Most expressions of defensiveness also give an impression of submissiveness.

Navigating the Hierarchy

Whether you're an owner, middle manager, supervisor, or an entry-level employee at the very bottom of the organizational chart, or somewhere in between, navigating the hierarchy of power and authority in your company is something that everyone must do.

Happy Employees = Happy Company

If you are an owner, manager, or supervisor, you have a vested interest in having a team of subordinates who are productive and satisfied in their positions. Numerous studies have been conducted to explore the relationship between employee satisfaction and engagement, employee productivity, and organizational success, and the results are clear that happy employees offer the best chances of having a happy, successful company.

One of the key components in the matrix of factors that influence and contribute to employee satisfaction is related to communication. Employees like to feel respected and appreciated by their superiors, even when they are in the lowest positions of the company. It is important to them to feel that they matter and that they are recognized and heard as individuals.

Lack of engagement and investment in the company and the work results in a decrease in productivity and increases the risk of such things as attending to personal matters while on company time, working at a slower pace than could or should be expected, delaying or refusing to do certain tasks, along with challenges to authority and other counter-productive behaviors, up to and including sabotage of professional objectives and the theft of company property.

While traditional or "hard" forms of compensation, such as pay, benefits, and opportunities for promotion and advancement invariably rank as the highest priority in contributing to employee satisfaction, the social, environmental, or "soft" conditions in a workplace play a more important role in employee engagement than many owners and managers recognize.

It has to be remembered that employees view themselves as people first, employees second. It is human nature to desire respect and respectful attention, to have a voice and to have that voice be heard and acknowledged. It can be particularly important in professional environments where there is a clearly delineated power differential and hierarchy of authority.

Effective, respectful, and productive communication efforts on the part of high-ranking individuals within a company can serve to prevent the development of a workplace environment that alienates employees and inspires these efforts of resistance and subtle, undermining rebellion.

Someone who has attained a high-ranking managerial position is undoubtedly in possession of good direct communication skills, as such skills are required for advancement in that area. Yet many professionals focus on direct verbal communication, on making the best choices in word usage and delivery, overlooking the power and impact of nonverbal communication. This is a surprising fact, given that 55% of the messages received and relayed in face-to-face dialogue are based on nonverbal cues.

Understanding nonverbal messages in others and being able to harness that form of communication yourself can improve your dialogue with your employees, increase their feeling of being heard and valued, which will, in turn, increase employee engagement, satisfaction, and buy-in, which will result in greater productivity. Improving your soft skills can benefit your bottom line.

Body Language in the Workplace

Body language can be a landscape filled with landmines, with even the smallest unintentional gestures giving off signals that alienate clients and customers, as well as subordinates, which damages morale and negatively influences productivity.

In Your Office

You are sitting behind your desk, meeting with a client or a current or prospective employee. Before anyone makes a motion or utters a word, there is already a power play at work. That position, being seated behind a desk, translates into a display of authority. If the desk is large and the distance between you and the person with whom you are meeting is great, it provides a feeling of distance and separation, and from the visitor's point of view, even one of intimidation. The modern-day equivalent of a throne is a tall business chair, perched behind a large, impressive desk.

When greeting and conversing with an employee in that context, it is important to remember that all sorts of messages are attached to the simple setting of your office and your—and your visitor's—position within it.

Exerting Dominance

If you are looking to assert or emphasize your authority, this is a good setting. If you are dealing with someone who is challenging your authority or over whom you need to exert power, then your best position is behind your desk. There are a number of body language expressions that you can utilize to further strengthen that position of power:

- Sit straight, with a strong posture, shoulders held up and firm with confidence, or
- Sit back, increasing the distance.
- Head should be held up and forward-facing, chin slightly raised, which also signifies strength and confidence.

Depending on what you are trying to achieve, arm and hand placement and activities can be significant.

- If you are reprimanding someone or being approached with an idea or explanation that you have an unfavorable view of, crossing your arms across your chest will give an unspoken indication of your firmness and lack of openness; it will say "you have to explain/sell/justify yourself" without you needing to articulate those words.
- If your view is only slightly unfavorable, but still firm in its negativity, clasping your hands together on the desk in front of you is a good posture to take.
- Be careful to remain sitting straight up or slightly back, however, as leaning forward position can signify an active interest in what the speaker is saying.

- You should maintain a neutral facial expression and steady eye contact. This is a cue not only in humans but also in animals, of dominance. If the subordinate returns the gesture or returns your steady gaze, be aware of the possibility that it is intended to challenge your authority. If possible, do not be the first one to break the contact, as it is likely to be perceived as a sign of weakness, of giving in and submitting. The subordinate should be the first to break the gaze.

If a subordinate returns a steady gaze, be aware that it may be intended to challenge your authority. Do not be the first one to break it.

Expressing Openness

If you are meeting with a client, superior, or someone you would like to either build a connection with or get something from, it is a good idea to step out from behind the desk and meet in a neutral and equal space. A conference table at which you can sit across from each other or in two chairs in front of your desk, or in another location in your office, would be the best setting. This will automatically signal that you are not attempting to use space to exert dominance.

If you are willing and able to meet with your visitor without a desk between you, do your best to maintain open body language and to be aware of his/her body language when determining how well the meeting and conversation is going.

- Keep your arms uncrossed and at a neutral or open position, hands unclenched.
- Maintain steady eye contact, with your eyes wide (not exaggerated) and eyebrows raised slightly to indicate openness and interest.
- If your visitor is a female, nodding your head up-and-down will be interpreted as a cue of interest and encouragement to continue. If your visitor is male, be careful not to nod in an affirmative way unless you wish to clearly signal agreement and assent.
- Tilting your head slightly to one side can further strengthen an impression of interest.
- If your visitor is exhibiting open body language, mirroring his/her pose and position can give the impression that you are in alignment and on the same page.

If you are unwilling and/or unable to meet with your welcome visitor without a desk between you, openness and receptivity can be signaled through how you position your arms and hands:

- If you are somewhat open to whatever is being presented to you, then your arms should rest on the desk in front of you, directly lined up with your shoulders—imagine a straight line between your shoulders and the tips of your fingers.
- If you are highly receptive to the person and conversation, looking to convey a significant degree of openness, then increase the amount of space between your arms, making a slightly wide, welcoming "v" with the reference points of your shoulders and hands.
- Keep your hands unclenched and your facial expression open.

Maintaining steady eye contact, avoiding clenching your hands, and keeping an open facial expression and body posture will convey interest and receptivity to your visitor.

Chapter 6 – Navigation: The World at Large

The understanding and techniques for reading personalities and the nonverbal signals of body language that you have acquired in the earlier chapters of this book can be applied to interactions with all of the people in your life, from family members and friends to acquaintances and people you encounter on the street and as you go about your daily routines.

You do not necessarily have to be close to, or engage, someone to read him/her. In fact, watching people in public places like shopping malls and airports can provide you with opportunities to practice your new people reading skills. Look to broaden your personal references of visual, postural, and behavioral messages by analyzing people whenever and wherever you come into contact them. Think of it as developing a personal dictionary of signals, expressions, and personality cues.

While you have learned the foundation of reading personalities and body language, there is another area of nonverbal communication and analysis that that has a particularly strong bearing on interactions with strangers and acquaintances in daily life, that of "proxemics," or what we most commonly think of and refer to as "personal space."

Proxemics

Whether or not you have ever thought about it in terms of feet and inches, you are likely to recognize that the distance at which someone stands from you in interpersonal exchanges affects your feeling about and response to the interaction. If someone stands too close, you can feel crowded and uncomfortable, almost even harassed or violated, depending upon your knowledge of and relationship with that person. Conversely, you are unconsciously aware of the negative message conveyed when someone you know well and intimately keeps at what seems too great of a distance when you are conversing with him or her.

Proxemics addresses this phenomenon through the identification of zones of acceptable proximity for different types of relationships and contexts. The zones are as follows:

The Four Zones

Intimate Zone

- **Range:** Between 6 inches/.5 foot and 18 inches/1.5 feet (or 15-45 cm).
- **Significance:** This is a person's private zone and most personal space, close enough that minute body features and qualities can be clearly viewed, smelled, or touched with ease. Because it is so close, so intimate, people tend to be very protective of it. Only those who are familiar and well-known are typically welcome in this zone, and if a stranger or a casual acquaintance crosses into it, the result will be a feeling of negativity and discomfort.
- **Welcomed:** Close family member and friends, spouses and lovers. Domestic pets are also welcomed into the intimate zone in most cases.

Personal Zone

- **Range:** Between 18 inches/1.5 feet and 48 inches/2 feet (or 46cm—1.22m).
- **Significance:** This is a zone for relatively close social interactions. It is enough of a distance for there to be a sense of being

personal with someone, without the implication of intimacy. It is close enough to facilitate some forms of physical contact, such as touching an arm to capture attention or express interest in something that someone is saying, but not so close as to invite feelings of impropriety. Most are comfortable with friends and colleagues occupying that space, but your individual relationship with someone will determine how comfortable you are with someone being in this zone.

- **Welcomed:** General friends, co-workers and colleagues, other attendees of certain social functions and gatherings.

Social Zone

Range: Between 4 feet and 12 feet (or 1.22 to 3.6m).

Significance: This is the zone where we expect those we have friendly social and practical relationships with, such as new co-workers and service workers like a postal carrier, plumber, or salesperson in the retail shop. There must be some foundation of knowing and being acquainted with those who can be in this zone without creating a feeling of discomfort or impropriety.

Welcomed: Those you are familiar with but do not know well, such as new and unfamiliar colleagues, people employed to do temporary work for you, workers in the service industry and customers in your workplace.

Public Zone

Range: 12 feet and beyond (or more than 3.6m).

Significance: This is the zone in which we prefer to greet and address strangers or those we are not acquainted with. If someone is teaching or giving a presentation, there is an expectation that those in the audience will keep this distance. On the street and out in the world, this is the preferred distance for people that we do not know.

Welcomed: Strangers, members of an audience, neighbors with whom we have had little-to-no direct and personal interaction.

Keeping Your Distance

It is important to recognize and honor these zones of contact and comfort, as crossing over into a more personal space when you do not possess a relationship that justifies that degree of proximity can not only distract the person to whom you are approaching but can also create feelings of being uncomfortable, "put upon," or even harassed or violated.

This can be a particularly tricky challenge to those with Extraverted (E) and Feeling (F) personality characteristics, as they have a natural drive and desire to get closer to people for better and more authentic communications. Those within the Intuitive-Feeling (NF), or Idealist, group type need to be especially careful of the acceptable degrees of proximity, as they want to connect with others on ever-more personal levels, to such an extent that they may not realize that they are undermining their efforts by infringing too close into someone's space until discomfort has already been established.

Extraverted and Feeling personality types, along with Intuitive Feeling "Idealists" need to exercise particular care in recognizing and respecting personal space, as they are more inclined to get closer than other types.

Introverts (N), Thinkers (T), and Judgers (J) are particularly conscious of—and protective of—personal zones of space, as they prefer a greater distance from others overall, often seeming aloof and distant even when they are at their most social level. If someone crosses too far into the personal or intimate zone of certain personality types, most notably the INTJ, who has three signifiers of preferring distance and space in interpersonal interactions, he/she cannot expect to communicate effectively, as the discomfort felt from the inappropriate proximity will overshadow any other messages that are being conveyed.

At the bottom line, space matters. Knowing someone's personality type can help you to determine the correct distance to keep in social interactions. If in doubt, it is best and safest to opt for a greater distance, rather than a closer one, and watch the individual for cues of a desire to get closer.

If someone physically steps back and away from you, under no circumstances should you respond by stepping forward to close the distance between you again, unless you want to engage in something of a chase around a room—or risk having someone break off the exchange entirely, fleeing to a space and interaction with another who will not crowd them.

Conclusion

We live in a diverse, multi-cultural, global society, populated with people who possess different—sometimes even dramatically so—viewpoints, perspectives, and opinions about life and the world. We all must coexist, cooperate, and interact with one another to forge and maintain productive relationships that, ideally, have a minimum of conflict.

There is no cookie cutter recipe for effective and constructive communication with everyone, however. There are no sweeping, across-the-board methods to ensure that interpersonal interactions always follow along desired lines and bring about desired results. The unique personalities, tendencies, and interactive styles that individuals possess make it necessary to scratch below the surface to truly understand a person before you can know the best way in which to communicate with him or her.

Unique personalities and interactive styles make it necessary to truly understand a person before you can know the best way in which to communicate with him or her.

That effort of scratching below the surface can be greatly improved by reading a person's personality style and analyzing the body language that everyone unconsciously conveys in their communication. This book has offered information, tools, and tips to assist in the effort of reading and understanding the nonverbal signals, signs, and cues that reveal not only personality but also mood, thoughts, feelings, motives, and intentions.

As mentioned early in this book, reading and communicating with people is a journey. Becoming familiar with the map of personality traits and types, along with a grasp of the nonverbal expressions of body language, provides you with the foundation of knowledge to better understand the people that you interact with in all spheres of life. That knowledge, combined with the practices of vigilant observation and analysis of context and expression clusters, will allow you to read people accurately and, with that greater understanding, communicate more effectively and productively.

Copyright 2019 by: Lawrence_Franz

All rights reserved.

This document is geared towards providing exact and reliable information in regards to the topic and issue covered. The publication is sold with the idea that the publisher is not required to render an accounting, officially permitted, or otherwise, qualified services. If advice is necessary, legal or professional, a practiced individual in the profession should be ordered.

- From a Declaration of Principles which was accepted and approved equally by a Committee of the American Bar Association and a Committee of Publishers and Associations.

In no way is it legal to reproduce, duplicate, or transmit any part of this document in either electronic means or in printed format. Recording of this publication is strictly prohibited and any storage of this document is not allowed unless with written permission from the publisher. All rights reserved.

The information provided herein is stated to be truthful and consistent, in that any liability, in terms of inattention or otherwise, by any usage or abuse of any policies, processes, or directions contained within is the solitary and utter responsibility of the recipient reader. Under no circumstances will any legal responsibility or blame be held against the publisher for any reparation, damages, or monetary loss due to the information herein, either directly or indirectly.

Respective authors own all copyrights not held by the publisher.

The information herein is offered for informational purposes solely and is universal as so. The presentation of the information is without a contract or any type of guarantee assurance.

The trademarks that are used are without any consent, and the publication of the trademark is without permission or backing by the trademark owner. All trademarks and brands within this book are for clarifying purposes only and are the owned by the owners themselves, not affiliated with this document.